WOLFSNAIL

A Backyard Predator

Sarah C. Campbell

Photographs by

Sarah C. Campbell and Richard P. Campbell

Boyds Mills Press

Honesdale, Pennsylvania

Acknowledgments

I owe many people a debt of thanks for their help in making this book possible: my parents, David and Patty Crosby, who have believed since the very first story; my husband, Richard, who taught me many things I needed to know about high-tech photography (and took the bird photograph for this book at the perfect moment); and my sons, who fueled my fascination for wolfsnails.

For their help with the science, I thank: Dr. Robert Jones, curator of invertebrates at the Mississippi Museum of Natural Science in Jackson, who first identified the snails; Dr. Melissa Harrington, associate professor of biotechnology at Delaware State University in Dover, who shared her neuroscience research on wolfsnails and taught me how to keep our snails alive; and Dr. Timothy Pearce, assistant curator and head of the mollusks section at the Carnegie Museum of Natural History in Pittsburgh, Pennsylvania, who reviewed the manuscript.

On the writing side, I thank my editor, Andy Boyles, who helped me find the story; and my colleagues in the Southern Breeze chapter of the Society of Children's Book Writers and Illustrators.

—S.C.C.

Text copyright © 2008 by Sarah C. Campbell
Photographs copyright © 2008 by Sarah C. Campbell and Richard P. Campbell

Boyds Mills Press, Inc.
815 Church Street
Honesdale, Pennsylvania 18431
Printed in the United States of America

Library of Congress Cataloging-in-Publication Data

Campbell, Sarah C.
  Wolfsnail : a backyard predator / written by Sarah C. Campbell ; photographs by Sarah C. Campbell and Richard P. Campbell. — 1st ed.
      p. cm.
  ISBN 978-1-59078-554-6 (hardcover : alk. paper)
  1. Rosy wolfsnail—Juvenile literature. I. Campbell, Richard P., ill. II. Title.

  QL430.5.S65C36 2008
  594'.38—dc22

                              2007030838

First edition
The text of this book is set in 24-point Optima.

10 9 8 7 6 5 4 3

Water from a spring rain
runs along the edge
of a porch.

It falls onto the shell of a wolfsnail.
The snail is tucked inside its shell.

Today, it is time to wake up and find food.
Water seeps into an opening in the shell.
The snail begins to move. Its tail comes out
first, then its head.

Soon the snail's long, slimy foot is
fully stretched out.

The wolfsnail glides along the ground
until it comes to the stem of a hosta plant.

It climbs up.
Does the wolfsnail bite into
a crisp hosta leaf?

No. Most land snails,
such as this one, eat plants.
The wolfsnail eats meat.

The wolfsnail glides along the hosta
in search of snails and slugs that
feed on its leaves.

Where are they?

The wolfsnail tracks its prey
using a special detection system.
Leaf-eating snails have just four
tentacles—a lower pair of feelers and
a higher pair with eyes at the ends.

A wolfsnail has these four tentacles plus a set of lip extensions. The snail looks like it has a mustache. The wolfsnail *tap, tap, taps* the top of the leaf, searching for signs of food.

When the wolfsnail finds a slime
trail, it knows that its prey is close
by. A slime trail is made from
mucus, which snails and slugs lay
down to grip and glide along all
kinds of surfaces.

The wolfsnail turns to follow the trail.

It moves faster than other snails.

Whoa! A shadow crosses the leaf. A bird lands nearby.

The wolfsnail retreats.
It stays still and waits.

All is quiet.

The wolfsnail resumes its hunt.

The wolfsnail finds its prey.

It grabs the snail,

lifts it up to expose the opening
in its shell, and attacks.

The wolfsnail bites into the smaller snail using the tiny teeth on its tongue. This toothy tongue is called a radula. When the prey snail retreats, the wolfsnail pushes its radula deep into the shell to finish its meal.

The wolfsnail leaves behind
an empty shell.

It is no longer hungry.
It climbs down the hosta

and glides along the soil.
Wait! Something else moves.

The wolfsnail ignores the worm.
It eats only snails and slugs.

The wolfsnail settles into a
cool spot under the porch ledge,
pulls its flesh into its shell,
and falls asleep.

WOLFSNAIL FACTS

The photographs in this book make the wolfsnail look much larger than it actually is. This photo shows the wolfsnail at its true size.

Scientific Name: *Euglandina rosea*

Common Names: rosy wolfsnail, cannibal snail

Size: Adult shells are approximately 1½ to 3 inches, or 4 to 7½ centimeters, long.

Distribution: This species is found naturally in the southeastern United States—in Alabama, Florida, Georgia, Louisiana, Mississippi, North Carolina, South Carolina, Tennessee, and Texas. Rosy wolfsnails were introduced into Hawaii in the 1950s in a failed attempt to control unwanted leaf-eating snails. Outside the United States, the rosy wolfsnail has also been introduced into American Samoa, Andaman Islands, the Bahamas, Bermuda, French Polynesia, Guam, Hong Kong, India, Japan, Kiribati, Madagascar, Mauritius, New Caledonia, Northern Mariana Islands, Papua New Guinea, Paulau, Réunion, Sabah, the Seychelles, Solomon Islands, Sri Lanka, Taiwan, and Vanuatu.

Habitat: moist undergrowth

Food: small garden snails, small slugs

Predators: birds, rats

Special characteristics: Most land snails are herbivores, or plant eaters. However, many snails that live in salt water are carnivores. Some other carnivorous land snails found in North America are the gray-foot lancetooth snail (*Haplotrema concavum*) and the decollate snail (*Rumina decollata*).

MORE ABOUT WOLFSNAILS

The wolfsnail in this story eats a snail and leaves the shell behind. When the prey snail is tiny, the wolfsnail eats the whole thing, shell and all. The wolfsnail also eats every bit of a slug. The wolfsnail absorbs calcium from the tiny snail shells it swallows whole and from the slugs' inner shells. It uses calcium to grow its own shell.

The wolfsnail uses its tracking system to find mates as well as prey. Like most other land snails, wolfsnails are hermaphrodites, or animals with both male and female body parts. This means that any wolfsnail is a potential mate for any other wolfsnail and that, after mating, both snails can lay eggs. During mating (pictured left) the snails remain locked together for hours.

Between three weeks and six months later, the wolfsnail lays eggs. Though many land snails dig shallow holes in the soil to lay their eggs, wolfsnails lay tiny white oval eggs, as many as twenty at a time, on top of the soil, usually under a leaf or a log. After laying the eggs, the wolfsnail moves on. About six weeks later, the eggs hatch, and the nearly transparent baby snails go immediately in search of food. It takes a few years of good eating and growing for a wolfsnail to reach adulthood.

State agricultural officials in Hawaii imported wolfsnails in 1955 to try to control another invader, the giant African snail, which was eating farmers' crops. But the wolfsnails ate native Hawaiian snails instead. Wolfsnails have wiped out many of the native snail species.

Snail Words

calcium a silvery metallic element that appears in shells and bones.

cannibal any animal that feeds on others of its own kind.

carnivore an animal that eats other animals.

herbivore an animal that eats plants.

hermaphrodite an animal with both male and female sex organs.

lip extensions sensory organs that are located at the base of the lower tentacles in rosy wolfsnails and some other predatory snails. They are shaped like a handlebar mustache.

mollusk an animal that has a soft body and is often enclosed in a hard shell. Snails, clams, and oysters are examples of mollusks.

mucus the slimy secretion that moistens and protects the foot of a slug or snail.

predator an animal that lives by killing and feeding on other animals.

prey an animal hunted for food by another animal.

radula a flexible, tonguelike organ, in snails and other mollusks, that has rows of teeth on the surface and is used in feeding.

slime moist, slippery mucus laid down as a snail or slug moves.

slug a small snail-like animal with no outer shell.

tentacle a long, slender, flexible growth at the head of a snail. The top two tentacles of most land snails have eyes at the tips. Both top and bottom tentacles are used for smelling and tasting.